MW01233582

mindful morning

date: June 18, 2021

TODAY I'M FEELING

optimistic
a little nervous
a little sad

5 THINGS I'M GRATEFUL FOR

My home
warm comfy bed
Audrey
My Health
Dependable transportation

DAILY AFFIRMATION

You are brave!

DAILY INTENTION

Concentrate on my
mental health.

mindful morning

date: June 19, 2021

TODAY I'M FEELING

Sad because Stuart isn't very supportive. A little shaky in my upper arms.

5 THINGS I'M GRATEFUL FOR

Barbara
My kids
My home
My vehicle
Opportunity for treatment

DAILY AFFIRMATION

You are brave and strong and getting better everyday.

DAILY INTENTION

Be present and patient.

mindful morning

date: June 20, 2021

TODAY I'M FEELING

tired
cautiously optimistic
little shaky

5 THINGS I'M GRATEFUL FOR

My inlaws
treatment
My family
My kids
Sally

DAILY AFFIRMATION

Jesus loves you and
made you special.

DAILY INTENTION

Be patient.

mindful morning

date: June 21, 2021

TODAY I'M FEELING

A little nervous.
Cautiously optimistic.

5 THINGS I'M GRATEFUL FOR

Stable home.
Husband who works.
Sally
Treatment
Good medical help.

DAILY AFFIRMATION

You are Worthy.

DAILY INTENTION

Be present and make
the most of today.

Be kind to
myself.

mindful morning

date:

TODAY I'M FEELING

Well rested
I have energy
I'm feeling positive

5 THINGS I'M GRATEFUL FOR

A good nights rest last night.
I am thankful for outpatient.
Im thankful Stuart is in town.
I am thankful for healthy kids.
I am thankful for Audrey.
I am thankful for God.

DAILY AFFIRMATION

I am going to conquer
this anxiety.

DAILY INTENTION

Be present at school
and at home.

mindful morning

date:

TODAY I'M FEELING

A little down.

5 THINGS I'M GRATEFUL FOR

Sally.
My kids.
My husband.
My home.
The ability to seek treatment
for anxiety.

DAILY AFFIRMATION

You are Strong!

DAILY INTENTION

Take a day for reflection.

mindful morning

date:

TODAY I'M FEELING

_____
_____
_____

5 THINGS I'M GRATEFUL FOR

_____
_____
_____
_____
_____

DAILY AFFIRMATION

_____
_____

DAILY INTENTION

_____
_____

mindful morning

date:

TODAY I'M FEELING

_____

_____

_____

5 THINGS I'M GRATEFUL FOR

_____

_____

_____

_____

_____

DAILY AFFIRMATION

_____

_____

DAILY INTENTION

_____

_____

mindful morning

date:

TODAY I'M FEELING

_____
_____
_____

5 THINGS I'M GRATEFUL FOR

_____
_____
_____
_____
_____

DAILY AFFIRMATION

_____
_____

DAILY INTENTION

_____
_____

mindful morning

date:

TODAY I'M FEELING

_____

_____

_____

5 THINGS I'M GRATEFUL FOR

_____

_____

_____

_____

_____

DAILY AFFIRMATION

_____

_____

DAILY INTENTION

_____

_____

mindful morning

date:

TODAY I'M FEELING

_____
_____
_____

5 THINGS I'M GRATEFUL FOR

_____
_____
_____
_____
_____

DAILY AFFIRMATION

_____
_____

DAILY INTENTION

_____
_____

mindful morning

date:

TODAY I'M FEELING

_____
_____
_____

5 THINGS I'M GRATEFUL FOR

_____
_____
_____
_____
_____

DAILY AFFIRMATION

_____
_____

DAILY INTENTION

_____
_____

mindful morning

date:

TODAY I'M FEELING

_____
_____
_____

5 THINGS I'M GRATEFUL FOR

_____
_____
_____
_____
_____

DAILY AFFIRMATION

_____
_____

DAILY INTENTION

_____
_____

mindful morning

date:

TODAY I'M FEELING

_____
_____
_____

5 THINGS I'M GRATEFUL FOR

_____
_____
_____
_____
_____

DAILY AFFIRMATION

_____
_____

DAILY INTENTION

_____
_____

mindful morning

date:

TODAY I'M FEELING

_____

_____

_____

5 THINGS I'M GRATEFUL FOR

_____

_____

_____

_____

_____

DAILY AFFIRMATION

_____

_____

DAILY INTENTION

_____

_____

mindful morning

date:

TODAY I'M FEELING

_____
_____
_____

5 THINGS I'M GRATEFUL FOR

_____
_____
_____
_____
_____

DAILY AFFIRMATION

_____
_____

DAILY INTENTION

_____
_____

mindful morning

date:

TODAY I'M FEELING

_____
_____
_____

5 THINGS I'M GRATEFUL FOR

_____
_____
_____
_____
_____

DAILY AFFIRMATION

_____
_____

DAILY INTENTION

_____
_____

mindful morning

date:

TODAY I'M FEELING

_____
_____
_____

5 THINGS I'M GRATEFUL FOR

_____
_____
_____
_____
_____

DAILY AFFIRMATION

_____
_____

DAILY INTENTION

_____
_____

mindful morning

date:

TODAY I'M FEELING

_____
_____
_____

5 THINGS I'M GRATEFUL FOR

_____
_____
_____
_____
_____

DAILY AFFIRMATION

_____
_____

DAILY INTENTION

_____
_____

mindful morning

date:

TODAY I'M FEELING

_____
_____
_____

5 THINGS I'M GRATEFUL FOR

_____
_____
_____
_____
_____

DAILY AFFIRMATION

_____
_____

DAILY INTENTION

_____
_____

mindful morning

date:

TODAY I'M FEELING

_____
_____
_____

5 THINGS I'M GRATEFUL FOR

_____
_____
_____
_____
_____

DAILY AFFIRMATION

_____
_____

DAILY INTENTION

_____
_____

mindful morning

date:

TODAY I'M FEELING

_____

_____

_____

5 THINGS I'M GRATEFUL FOR

_____

_____

_____

_____

_____

DAILY AFFIRMATION

_____

_____

DAILY INTENTION

_____

_____

mindful morning

date:

TODAY I'M FEELING

_____
_____
_____

5 THINGS I'M GRATEFUL FOR

_____
_____
_____
_____
_____

DAILY AFFIRMATION

_____
_____

DAILY INTENTION

_____
_____

mindful morning

date:

TODAY I'M FEELING

_____
_____
_____

5 THINGS I'M GRATEFUL FOR

_____
_____
_____
_____
_____

DAILY AFFIRMATION

_____
_____

DAILY INTENTION

_____
_____

mindful morning

date:

TODAY I'M FEELING

_____
_____
_____

5 THINGS I'M GRATEFUL FOR

_____
_____
_____
_____
_____

DAILY AFFIRMATION

_____
_____

DAILY INTENTION

_____
_____

mindful morning

date:

TODAY I'M FEELING

_____
_____
_____

5 THINGS I'M GRATEFUL FOR

_____
_____
_____
_____
_____

DAILY AFFIRMATION

_____
_____

DAILY INTENTION

_____
_____

mindful morning

date:

TODAY I'M FEELING

_____
_____
_____

5 THINGS I'M GRATEFUL FOR

_____
_____
_____
_____
_____

DAILY AFFIRMATION

_____
_____

DAILY INTENTION

_____
_____

mindful morning

date:

TODAY I'M FEELING

_____

_____

_____

5 THINGS I'M GRATEFUL FOR

_____

_____

_____

_____

_____

DAILY AFFIRMATION

_____

_____

DAILY INTENTION

_____

_____

mindful morning

date:

TODAY I'M FEELING

_____
_____
_____

5 THINGS I'M GRATEFUL FOR

_____
_____
_____
_____

DAILY AFFIRMATION

_____
_____

DAILY INTENTION

_____
_____

mindful morning

date:

TODAY I'M FEELING

_____
_____
_____

5 THINGS I'M GRATEFUL FOR

_____
_____
_____
_____
_____

DAILY AFFIRMATION

_____
_____

DAILY INTENTION

_____
_____

mindful morning

date:

TODAY I'M FEELING

_____
_____
_____

5 THINGS I'M GRATEFUL FOR

_____
_____
_____
_____
_____

DAILY AFFIRMATION

_____
_____

DAILY INTENTION

_____
_____

mindful morning

date:

TODAY I'M FEELING

_____
_____
_____

5 THINGS I'M GRATEFUL FOR

_____
_____
_____
_____
_____

DAILY AFFIRMATION

_____
_____

DAILY INTENTION

_____
_____

mindful morning

date:

TODAY I'M FEELING

_____
_____
_____

5 THINGS I'M GRATEFUL FOR

_____
_____
_____
_____
_____

DAILY AFFIRMATION

_____
_____

DAILY INTENTION

_____
_____

mindful morning

date:

TODAY I'M FEELING

_____
_____
_____

5 THINGS I'M GRATEFUL FOR

_____
_____
_____
_____
_____

DAILY AFFIRMATION

_____
_____

DAILY INTENTION

_____
_____

mindful morning

date:

TODAY I'M FEELING

_____
_____
_____

5 THINGS I'M GRATEFUL FOR

_____
_____
_____
_____
_____

DAILY AFFIRMATION

_____
_____

DAILY INTENTION

_____
_____

mindful morning

date:

TODAY I'M FEELING

_____
_____
_____

5 THINGS I'M GRATEFUL FOR

_____
_____
_____
_____
_____

DAILY AFFIRMATION

_____
_____

DAILY INTENTION

_____
_____

mindful morning

date:

TODAY I'M FEELING

_____
_____
_____

5 THINGS I'M GRATEFUL FOR

_____
_____
_____
_____
_____

DAILY AFFIRMATION

_____
_____

DAILY INTENTION

_____
_____

mindful morning

date:

TODAY I'M FEELING

_____
_____
_____

5 THINGS I'M GRATEFUL FOR

_____
_____
_____
_____
_____

DAILY AFFIRMATION

_____
_____

DAILY INTENTION

_____
_____

mindful morning

date:

TODAY I'M FEELING

_____
_____
_____

5 THINGS I'M GRATEFUL FOR

_____
_____
_____
_____
_____

DAILY AFFIRMATION

_____
_____

DAILY INTENTION

_____
_____

mindful morning

date:

TODAY I'M FEELING

_____
_____
_____

5 THINGS I'M GRATEFUL FOR

_____
_____
_____
_____
_____

DAILY AFFIRMATION

_____
_____

DAILY INTENTION

_____
_____

mindful morning

date:

TODAY I'M FEELING

_____

_____

_____

5 THINGS I'M GRATEFUL FOR

_____

_____

_____

_____

_____

DAILY AFFIRMATION

_____

_____

DAILY INTENTION

_____

_____

mindful morning

date:

TODAY I'M FEELING

_____

_____

_____

5 THINGS I'M GRATEFUL FOR

_____

_____

_____

_____

_____

DAILY AFFIRMATION

_____

_____

DAILY INTENTION

_____

_____

mindful morning

date:

TODAY I'M FEELING

_____
_____
_____

5 THINGS I'M GRATEFUL FOR

_____
_____
_____
_____
_____

DAILY AFFIRMATION

_____
_____

DAILY INTENTION

_____
_____

mindful morning

date:

TODAY I'M FEELING

_____
_____
_____

5 THINGS I'M GRATEFUL FOR

_____
_____
_____
_____
_____

DAILY AFFIRMATION

_____
_____

DAILY INTENTION

_____
_____

mindful morning

date:

TODAY I'M FEELING

_____
_____
_____

5 THINGS I'M GRATEFUL FOR

_____
_____
_____
_____
_____

DAILY AFFIRMATION

_____
_____

DAILY INTENTION

_____
_____

mindful morning

date:

TODAY I'M FEELING

_____
_____
_____

5 THINGS I'M GRATEFUL FOR

_____
_____
_____
_____
_____

DAILY AFFIRMATION

_____
_____

DAILY INTENTION

_____
_____

mindful morning

date: _____

TODAY I'M FEELING

_____
_____
_____

5 THINGS I'M GRATEFUL FOR

_____
_____
_____
_____
_____

DAILY AFFIRMATION

_____
_____

DAILY INTENTION

_____
_____

mindful morning

date:

TODAY I'M FEELING

_____
_____
_____

5 THINGS I'M GRATEFUL FOR

_____
_____
_____
_____
_____

DAILY AFFIRMATION

_____
_____

DAILY INTENTION

_____
_____

mindful morning

date:

TODAY I'M FEELING

_____
_____
_____

5 THINGS I'M GRATEFUL FOR

_____
_____
_____
_____
_____

DAILY AFFIRMATION

_____

DAILY INTENTION

_____

mindful morning

date:

TODAY I'M FEELING

_____
_____
_____

5 THINGS I'M GRATEFUL FOR

_____
_____
_____
_____
_____

DAILY AFFIRMATION

_____
_____

DAILY INTENTION

_____
_____

mindful morning

date:

TODAY I'M FEELING

_____
_____
_____

5 THINGS I'M GRATEFUL FOR

_____
_____
_____
_____
_____

DAILY AFFIRMATION

_____
_____

DAILY INTENTION

_____
_____

mindful morning

date:

TODAY I'M FEELING

_____
_____
_____

5 THINGS I'M GRATEFUL FOR

_____
_____
_____
_____
_____

DAILY AFFIRMATION

_____
_____

DAILY INTENTION

_____
_____

mindful morning

date:

TODAY I'M FEELING

_____

_____

_____

5 THINGS I'M GRATEFUL FOR

_____

_____

_____

_____

_____

DAILY AFFIRMATION

_____

DAILY INTENTION

_____

_____

mindful morning

date:

TODAY I'M FEELING

_____

_____

_____

5 THINGS I'M GRATEFUL FOR

_____

_____

_____

_____

_____

DAILY AFFIRMATION

_____

_____

DAILY INTENTION

_____

_____

mindful morning

date:

TODAY I'M FEELING

_____

_____

_____

5 THINGS I'M GRATEFUL FOR

_____

_____

_____

_____

_____

DAILY AFFIRMATION

_____

DAILY INTENTION

_____

mindful morning

date:

TODAY I'M FEELING

_____
_____
_____

5 THINGS I'M GRATEFUL FOR

_____
_____
_____
_____
_____

DAILY AFFIRMATION

_____
_____

DAILY INTENTION

_____
_____

mindful morning

date:

TODAY I'M FEELING

_____

_____

_____

5 THINGS I'M GRATEFUL FOR

_____

_____

_____

_____

_____

DAILY AFFIRMATION

_____

_____

DAILY INTENTION

_____

_____

mindful morning

date:

TODAY I'M FEELING

_____
_____
_____

5 THINGS I'M GRATEFUL FOR

_____
_____
_____
_____
_____

DAILY AFFIRMATION

_____
_____

DAILY INTENTION

_____
_____

mindful morning

date:

TODAY I'M FEELING

_____
_____
_____

5 THINGS I'M GRATEFUL FOR

_____
_____
_____
_____
_____

DAILY AFFIRMATION

_____

DAILY INTENTION

_____
_____

mindful morning

date:

TODAY I'M FEELING

_____
_____
_____

5 THINGS I'M GRATEFUL FOR

_____
_____
_____
_____
_____

DAILY AFFIRMATION

_____
_____

DAILY INTENTION

_____
_____

mindful morning

date:

TODAY I'M FEELING

_____
_____
_____

5 THINGS I'M GRATEFUL FOR

_____
_____
_____
_____
_____

DAILY AFFIRMATION

_____
_____

DAILY INTENTION

_____
_____

mindful morning

date:

TODAY I'M FEELING

_____
_____
_____

5 THINGS I'M GRATEFUL FOR

_____
_____
_____
_____
_____

DAILY AFFIRMATION

_____
_____

DAILY INTENTION

_____
_____

mindful morning

date:

TODAY I'M FEELING

_____
_____
_____

5 THINGS I'M GRATEFUL FOR

_____
_____
_____
_____
_____

DAILY AFFIRMATION

_____

DAILY INTENTION

_____

mindful morning

date:

TODAY I'M FEELING

_____
_____
_____

5 THINGS I'M GRATEFUL FOR

_____
_____
_____
_____
_____

DAILY AFFIRMATION

_____
_____

DAILY INTENTION

_____
_____

mindful morning

date:

TODAY I'M FEELING

_____
_____
_____

5 THINGS I'M GRATEFUL FOR

_____
_____
_____
_____
_____

DAILY AFFIRMATION

_____
_____

DAILY INTENTION

_____
_____

mindful morning

date: _____

TODAY I'M FEELING

_____
_____
_____

5 THINGS I'M GRATEFUL FOR

_____
_____
_____
_____
_____

DAILY AFFIRMATION

_____
_____

DAILY INTENTION

_____
_____

mindful morning

date:

TODAY I'M FEELING

_____
_____
_____

5 THINGS I'M GRATEFUL FOR

_____
_____
_____
_____
_____

DAILY AFFIRMATION

_____
_____

DAILY INTENTION

_____
_____

mindful morning

date:

TODAY I'M FEELING

_____
_____
_____

5 THINGS I'M GRATEFUL FOR

_____
_____
_____
_____
_____

DAILY AFFIRMATION

_____
_____

DAILY INTENTION

_____
_____

mindful morning

date:

TODAY I'M FEELING

_____
_____
_____

5 THINGS I'M GRATEFUL FOR

_____
_____
_____
_____
_____

DAILY AFFIRMATION

_____
_____

DAILY INTENTION

_____
_____

mindful morning

date:

TODAY I'M FEELING

_____
_____
_____

5 THINGS I'M GRATEFUL FOR

_____
_____
_____
_____
_____

DAILY AFFIRMATION

_____
_____

DAILY INTENTION

_____
_____

mindful morning

date:

TODAY I'M FEELING

_____
_____
_____

5 THINGS I'M GRATEFUL FOR

_____
_____
_____
_____
_____

DAILY AFFIRMATION

_____
_____

DAILY INTENTION

_____
_____

mindful morning

date:

TODAY I'M FEELING

_____

_____

_____

5 THINGS I'M GRATEFUL FOR

_____

_____

_____

_____

_____

DAILY AFFIRMATION

_____

_____

DAILY INTENTION

_____

_____

mindful morning

date:

TODAY I'M FEELING

_____
_____
_____

5 THINGS I'M GRATEFUL FOR

_____
_____
_____
_____
_____

DAILY AFFIRMATION

_____
_____

DAILY INTENTION

_____
_____

mindful morning

date:

TODAY I'M FEELING

_____
_____
_____

5 THINGS I'M GRATEFUL FOR

_____
_____
_____
_____
_____

DAILY AFFIRMATION

_____
_____

DAILY INTENTION

_____
_____

mindful morning

date:

TODAY I'M FEELING

_____
_____
_____

5 THINGS I'M GRATEFUL FOR

_____
_____
_____
_____
_____

DAILY AFFIRMATION

_____
_____

DAILY INTENTION

_____
_____

mindful morning

date:

TODAY I'M FEELING

_____
_____
_____

5 THINGS I'M GRATEFUL FOR

_____
_____
_____
_____
_____

DAILY AFFIRMATION

_____
_____

DAILY INTENTION

_____
_____

mindful morning

date:

TODAY I'M FEELING

_____
_____
_____

5 THINGS I'M GRATEFUL FOR

_____
_____
_____
_____
_____

DAILY AFFIRMATION

_____
_____

DAILY INTENTION

_____
_____

mindful morning

date:

TODAY I'M FEELING

_____
_____
_____

5 THINGS I'M GRATEFUL FOR

_____
_____
_____
_____
_____

DAILY AFFIRMATION

_____
_____

DAILY INTENTION

_____
_____

mindful morning

date:

TODAY I'M FEELING

_____
_____
_____

5 THINGS I'M GRATEFUL FOR

_____
_____
_____
_____
_____

DAILY AFFIRMATION

_____
_____

DAILY INTENTION

_____
_____

mindful morning

date:

TODAY I'M FEELING

_____
_____
_____

5 THINGS I'M GRATEFUL FOR

_____
_____
_____
_____
_____

DAILY AFFIRMATION

_____
_____

DAILY INTENTION

_____
_____

mindful morning

date:

TODAY I'M FEELING

_____
_____
_____

5 THINGS I'M GRATEFUL FOR

_____
_____
_____
_____
_____

DAILY AFFIRMATION

_____
_____

DAILY INTENTION

_____
_____

mindful morning

date:

TODAY I'M FEELING

_____

_____

_____

5 THINGS I'M GRATEFUL FOR

_____

_____

_____

_____

_____

DAILY AFFIRMATION

_____

_____

DAILY INTENTION

_____

_____

mindful morning

date:

TODAY I'M FEELING

_____
_____
_____

5 THINGS I'M GRATEFUL FOR

_____
_____
_____
_____
_____

DAILY AFFIRMATION

_____
_____

DAILY INTENTION

_____
_____

mindful morning

date:

TODAY I'M FEELING

_____

_____

_____

5 THINGS I'M GRATEFUL FOR

_____

_____

_____

_____

_____

DAILY AFFIRMATION

_____

_____

DAILY INTENTION

_____

_____

mindful morning

date:

TODAY I'M FEELING

_____
_____
_____

5 THINGS I'M GRATEFUL FOR

_____
_____
_____
_____
_____

DAILY AFFIRMATION

_____
_____

DAILY INTENTION

_____
_____

mindful morning

date:

TODAY I'M FEELING

_____
_____
_____

5 THINGS I'M GRATEFUL FOR

_____
_____
_____
_____
_____

DAILY AFFIRMATION

_____
_____

DAILY INTENTION

_____
_____

mindful morning

date:

TODAY I'M FEELING

_____
_____
_____

5 THINGS I'M GRATEFUL FOR

_____
_____
_____
_____
_____

DAILY AFFIRMATION

_____
_____

DAILY INTENTION

_____
_____

mindful morning

date:

TODAY I'M FEELING

_____
_____
_____

5 THINGS I'M GRATEFUL FOR

_____
_____
_____
_____
_____

DAILY AFFIRMATION

_____
_____

DAILY INTENTION

_____
_____

mindful morning

date:

TODAY I'M FEELING

_____
_____
_____

5 THINGS I'M GRATEFUL FOR

_____
_____
_____
_____
_____

DAILY AFFIRMATION

_____
_____

DAILY INTENTION

_____
_____

mindful morning

date:

TODAY I'M FEELING

_____
_____
_____

5 THINGS I'M GRATEFUL FOR

_____
_____
_____
_____
_____

DAILY AFFIRMATION

_____
_____

DAILY INTENTION

_____
_____

mindful morning

date:

TODAY I'M FEELING

_____
_____
_____

5 THINGS I'M GRATEFUL FOR

_____
_____
_____
_____
_____

DAILY AFFIRMATION

_____
_____

DAILY INTENTION

_____
_____

mindful morning

date:

TODAY I'M FEELING

_____
_____
_____

5 THINGS I'M GRATEFUL FOR

_____
_____
_____
_____
_____

DAILY AFFIRMATION

_____
_____

DAILY INTENTION

_____
_____

mindful morning

date:

TODAY I'M FEELING

_____
_____
_____

5 THINGS I'M GRATEFUL FOR

_____
_____
_____
_____
_____

DAILY AFFIRMATION

_____
_____

DAILY INTENTION

_____
_____

mindful morning

date:

TODAY I'M FEELING

_____
_____
_____

5 THINGS I'M GRATEFUL FOR

_____
_____
_____
_____
_____

DAILY AFFIRMATION

_____
_____

DAILY INTENTION

_____
_____

mindful morning

date:

TODAY I'M FEELING

_____
_____
_____

5 THINGS I'M GRATEFUL FOR

_____
_____
_____
_____
_____

DAILY AFFIRMATION

_____
_____

DAILY INTENTION

_____
_____

mindful morning

date:

TODAY I'M FEELING

_____
_____
_____

5 THINGS I'M GRATEFUL FOR

_____
_____
_____
_____
_____

DAILY AFFIRMATION

_____
_____

DAILY INTENTION

_____
_____

mindful morning

date:

TODAY I'M FEELING

_____
_____
_____

5 THINGS I'M GRATEFUL FOR

_____
_____
_____
_____
_____

DAILY AFFIRMATION

_____
_____

DAILY INTENTION

_____
_____

mindful morning

date:

TODAY I'M FEELING

_____
_____
_____

5 THINGS I'M GRATEFUL FOR

_____
_____
_____
_____
_____

DAILY AFFIRMATION

_____
_____

DAILY INTENTION

_____
_____

mindful morning

date:

TODAY I'M FEELING

_____
_____
_____

5 THINGS I'M GRATEFUL FOR

_____
_____
_____
_____
_____

DAILY AFFIRMATION

_____
_____

DAILY INTENTION

_____
_____

mindful morning

date:

TODAY I'M FEELING

_____
_____
_____

5 THINGS I'M GRATEFUL FOR

_____
_____
_____
_____
_____

DAILY AFFIRMATION

_____
_____

DAILY INTENTION

_____
_____

mindful morning

date:

TODAY I'M FEELING

_____
_____
_____

5 THINGS I'M GRATEFUL FOR

_____
_____
_____
_____
_____

DAILY AFFIRMATION

_____
_____

DAILY INTENTION

_____
_____

mindful morning

date:

TODAY I'M FEELING

_____
_____
_____

5 THINGS I'M GRATEFUL FOR

_____
_____
_____
_____
_____

DAILY AFFIRMATION

_____
_____

DAILY INTENTION

_____
_____

mindful morning

date:

TODAY I'M FEELING

_____
_____
_____

5 THINGS I'M GRATEFUL FOR

_____
_____
_____
_____
_____

DAILY AFFIRMATION

_____
_____

DAILY INTENTION

_____
_____

mindful morning

date:

TODAY I'M FEELING

_____

_____

_____

5 THINGS I'M GRATEFUL FOR

_____

_____

_____

_____

_____

DAILY AFFIRMATION

_____

_____

DAILY INTENTION

_____

_____

mindful morning

date:

TODAY I'M FEELING

_____
_____
_____

5 THINGS I'M GRATEFUL FOR

_____
_____
_____
_____
_____

DAILY AFFIRMATION

_____
_____

DAILY INTENTION

_____
_____

mindful morning

date:

TODAY I'M FEELING

_____
_____
_____

5 THINGS I'M GRATEFUL FOR

_____
_____
_____
_____
_____

DAILY AFFIRMATION

_____
_____

DAILY INTENTION

_____
_____

mindful morning

date:

TODAY I'M FEELING

_____
_____
_____

5 THINGS I'M GRATEFUL FOR

_____
_____
_____
_____
_____

DAILY AFFIRMATION

_____
_____

DAILY INTENTION

_____
_____

mindful morning

date: _____

TODAY I'M FEELING

_____
_____
_____

5 THINGS I'M GRATEFUL FOR

_____
_____
_____
_____
_____

DAILY AFFIRMATION

_____
_____

DAILY INTENTION

_____
_____

mindful morning

date:

TODAY I'M FEELING

_____
_____
_____

5 THINGS I'M GRATEFUL FOR

_____
_____
_____
_____
_____

DAILY AFFIRMATION

_____
_____

DAILY INTENTION

_____
_____

mindful morning

date:

TODAY I'M FEELING

_____
_____
_____

5 THINGS I'M GRATEFUL FOR

_____
_____
_____
_____
_____

DAILY AFFIRMATION

_____
_____

DAILY INTENTION

_____
_____

mindful morning

date:

TODAY I'M FEELING

_____
_____
_____

5 THINGS I'M GRATEFUL FOR

_____
_____
_____
_____
_____

DAILY AFFIRMATION

_____
_____

DAILY INTENTION

_____
_____

mindful morning

date:

TODAY I'M FEELING

_____
_____
_____

5 THINGS I'M GRATEFUL FOR

_____
_____
_____
_____
_____

DAILY AFFIRMATION

_____
_____

DAILY INTENTION

_____
_____

mindful morning

date:

TODAY I'M FEELING

_____
_____
_____

5 THINGS I'M GRATEFUL FOR

_____
_____
_____
_____
_____

DAILY AFFIRMATION

_____
_____

DAILY INTENTION

_____
_____

mindful morning

date:

TODAY I'M FEELING

_____
_____
_____

5 THINGS I'M GRATEFUL FOR

_____
_____
_____
_____
_____

DAILY AFFIRMATION

_____
_____

DAILY INTENTION

_____
_____

mindful morning

date:

TODAY I'M FEELING

_____

_____

_____

5 THINGS I'M GRATEFUL FOR

_____

_____

_____

_____

_____

DAILY AFFIRMATION

_____

_____

DAILY INTENTION

_____

_____

mindful morning

date:

TODAY I'M FEELING

_____
_____
_____

5 THINGS I'M GRATEFUL FOR

_____
_____
_____
_____
_____

DAILY AFFIRMATION

_____
_____

DAILY INTENTION

_____
_____

mindful morning

date:

TODAY I'M FEELING

_____
_____
_____

5 THINGS I'M GRATEFUL FOR

_____
_____
_____
_____
_____

DAILY AFFIRMATION

_____
_____

DAILY INTENTION

_____
_____

mindful morning

date:

TODAY I'M FEELING

_____
_____
_____

5 THINGS I'M GRATEFUL FOR

_____
_____
_____
_____
_____

DAILY AFFIRMATION

_____
_____

DAILY INTENTION

_____
_____

mindful morning

date:

TODAY I'M FEELING

_____
_____
_____

5 THINGS I'M GRATEFUL FOR

_____
_____
_____
_____
_____

DAILY AFFIRMATION

_____
_____

DAILY INTENTION

_____
_____

mindful morning

date:

TODAY I'M FEELING

_____
_____
_____

5 THINGS I'M GRATEFUL FOR

_____
_____
_____
_____
_____

DAILY AFFIRMATION

_____
_____

DAILY INTENTION

_____
_____

mindful morning

date:

TODAY I'M FEELING

_____
_____
_____

5 THINGS I'M GRATEFUL FOR

_____
_____
_____
_____
_____

DAILY AFFIRMATION

_____
_____

DAILY INTENTION

_____
_____

mindful morning

date:

TODAY I'M FEELING

_____

_____

_____

5 THINGS I'M GRATEFUL FOR

_____

_____

_____

_____

_____

DAILY AFFIRMATION

_____

_____

DAILY INTENTION

_____

_____

mindful morning

date:

TODAY I'M FEELING

_____
_____
_____

5 THINGS I'M GRATEFUL FOR

_____
_____
_____
_____
_____

DAILY AFFIRMATION

_____

DAILY INTENTION

_____

mindful morning

date:

TODAY I'M FEELING

_____
_____
_____

5 THINGS I'M GRATEFUL FOR

_____
_____
_____
_____
_____

DAILY AFFIRMATION

_____
_____

DAILY INTENTION

_____
_____

mindful morning

date:

TODAY I'M FEELING

_____
_____
_____

5 THINGS I'M GRATEFUL FOR

_____
_____
_____
_____
_____

DAILY AFFIRMATION

_____
_____

DAILY INTENTION

_____
_____

mindful morning

date:

TODAY I'M FEELING

_____
_____
_____

5 THINGS I'M GRATEFUL FOR

_____
_____
_____
_____
_____

DAILY AFFIRMATION

_____
_____

DAILY INTENTION

_____
_____

mindful morning

date:

TODAY I'M FEELING

_____
_____
_____

5 THINGS I'M GRATEFUL FOR

_____
_____
_____
_____
_____

DAILY AFFIRMATION

_____
_____

DAILY INTENTION

_____
_____

mindful morning

date:

TODAY I'M FEELING

_____
_____
_____

5 THINGS I'M GRATEFUL FOR

_____
_____
_____
_____
_____

DAILY AFFIRMATION

_____
_____

DAILY INTENTION

_____
_____

mindful morning

date:

TODAY I'M FEELING

_____
_____
_____

5 THINGS I'M GRATEFUL FOR

_____
_____
_____
_____
_____

DAILY AFFIRMATION

_____
_____

DAILY INTENTION

_____
_____

mindful morning

date:

TODAY I'M FEELING

_____
_____
_____

5 THINGS I'M GRATEFUL FOR

_____
_____
_____
_____
_____

DAILY AFFIRMATION

_____
_____

DAILY INTENTION

_____
_____

mindful morning

date:

TODAY I'M FEELING

_____
_____
_____

5 THINGS I'M GRATEFUL FOR

_____
_____
_____
_____
_____

DAILY AFFIRMATION

_____
_____

DAILY INTENTION

_____
_____

mindful morning

date:

TODAY I'M FEELING

_____
_____
_____

5 THINGS I'M GRATEFUL FOR

_____
_____
_____
_____
_____

DAILY AFFIRMATION

_____
_____

DAILY INTENTION

_____
_____

mindful morning

date:

TODAY I'M FEELING

_____
_____
_____

5 THINGS I'M GRATEFUL FOR

_____
_____
_____
_____
_____

DAILY AFFIRMATION

_____
_____

DAILY INTENTION

_____
_____

mindful morning

date:

TODAY I'M FEELING

_____
_____
_____

5 THINGS I'M GRATEFUL FOR

_____
_____
_____
_____
_____

DAILY AFFIRMATION

_____
_____

DAILY INTENTION

_____
_____

mindful morning

date:

TODAY I'M FEELING

_____
_____
_____

5 THINGS I'M GRATEFUL FOR

_____
_____
_____
_____
_____

DAILY AFFIRMATION

_____
_____

DAILY INTENTION

_____
_____

mindful morning

date:

TODAY I'M FEELING

_____

_____

_____

5 THINGS I'M GRATEFUL FOR

_____

_____

_____

_____

_____

DAILY AFFIRMATION

_____

_____

DAILY INTENTION

_____

_____

mindful morning

date:

TODAY I'M FEELING

_____

_____

_____

5 THINGS I'M GRATEFUL FOR

_____

_____

_____

_____

_____

DAILY AFFIRMATION

_____

_____

DAILY INTENTION

_____

_____

mindful morning

date:

TODAY I'M FEELING

_____

_____

_____

5 THINGS I'M GRATEFUL FOR

_____

_____

_____

_____

_____

DAILY AFFIRMATION

_____

_____

DAILY INTENTION

_____

_____

mindful morning

date:

TODAY I'M FEELING

_____
_____
_____

5 THINGS I'M GRATEFUL FOR

_____
_____
_____
_____
_____

DAILY AFFIRMATION

_____
_____

DAILY INTENTION

_____
_____

mindful morning

date:

TODAY I'M FEELING

_____
_____
_____

5 THINGS I'M GRATEFUL FOR

_____
_____
_____
_____
_____

DAILY AFFIRMATION

_____
_____

DAILY INTENTION

_____
_____

mindful morning

date:

TODAY I'M FEELING

_____
_____
_____

5 THINGS I'M GRATEFUL FOR

_____
_____
_____
_____
_____

DAILY AFFIRMATION

_____
_____

DAILY INTENTION

_____
_____

mindful morning

date:

TODAY I'M FEELING

_____
_____
_____

5 THINGS I'M GRATEFUL FOR

_____
_____
_____
_____
_____

DAILY AFFIRMATION

_____
_____

DAILY INTENTION

_____
_____

mindful morning

date:

TODAY I'M FEELING

_____
_____
_____

5 THINGS I'M GRATEFUL FOR

_____
_____
_____
_____
_____

DAILY AFFIRMATION

_____
_____

DAILY INTENTION

_____
_____

mindful morning

date:

TODAY I'M FEELING

_____
_____
_____

5 THINGS I'M GRATEFUL FOR

_____
_____
_____
_____
_____

DAILY AFFIRMATION

_____
_____

DAILY INTENTION

_____
_____

mindful morning

date:

TODAY I'M FEELING

_____
_____
_____

5 THINGS I'M GRATEFUL FOR

_____
_____
_____
_____
_____

DAILY AFFIRMATION

_____
_____

DAILY INTENTION

_____
_____

mindful morning

date:

TODAY I'M FEELING

_____
_____
_____

5 THINGS I'M GRATEFUL FOR

_____
_____
_____
_____
_____

DAILY AFFIRMATION

_____
_____

DAILY INTENTION

_____
_____

mindful morning

date:

TODAY I'M FEELING

_____
_____
_____

5 THINGS I'M GRATEFUL FOR

_____
_____
_____
_____
_____

DAILY AFFIRMATION

_____
_____

DAILY INTENTION

_____
_____

mindful morning

date:

TODAY I'M FEELING

_____
_____
_____

5 THINGS I'M GRATEFUL FOR

_____
_____
_____
_____
_____

DAILY AFFIRMATION

_____
_____

DAILY INTENTION

_____
_____

mindful morning

date:

TODAY I'M FEELING

_____
_____
_____

5 THINGS I'M GRATEFUL FOR

_____
_____
_____
_____
_____

DAILY AFFIRMATION

_____
_____

DAILY INTENTION

_____
_____

mindful morning

date:

TODAY I'M FEELING

_____

_____

_____

5 THINGS I'M GRATEFUL FOR

_____

_____

_____

_____

_____

DAILY AFFIRMATION

_____

_____

DAILY INTENTION

_____

_____

mindful morning

date:

TODAY I'M FEELING

_____
_____
_____

5 THINGS I'M GRATEFUL FOR

_____
_____
_____
_____
_____

DAILY AFFIRMATION

_____
_____

DAILY INTENTION

_____
_____

mindful morning

date:

TODAY I'M FEELING

_____
_____
_____

5 THINGS I'M GRATEFUL FOR

_____
_____
_____
_____
_____

DAILY AFFIRMATION

_____
_____

DAILY INTENTION

_____
_____

mindful morning

date:

TODAY I'M FEELING

_____
_____
_____

5 THINGS I'M GRATEFUL FOR

_____
_____
_____
_____
_____

DAILY AFFIRMATION

_____
_____

DAILY INTENTION

_____
_____

mindful morning

date:

TODAY I'M FEELING

_____
_____
_____

5 THINGS I'M GRATEFUL FOR

_____
_____
_____
_____
_____

DAILY AFFIRMATION

_____
_____

DAILY INTENTION

_____
_____

mindful morning

date:

TODAY I'M FEELING

_____
_____
_____

5 THINGS I'M GRATEFUL FOR

_____
_____
_____
_____
_____

DAILY AFFIRMATION

_____
_____

DAILY INTENTION

_____
_____

mindful morning

date:

TODAY I'M FEELING

_____
_____
_____

5 THINGS I'M GRATEFUL FOR

_____
_____
_____
_____
_____

DAILY AFFIRMATION

_____
_____

DAILY INTENTION

_____
_____

mindful morning

date:

TODAY I'M FEELING

_____
_____
_____

5 THINGS I'M GRATEFUL FOR

_____
_____
_____
_____
_____

DAILY AFFIRMATION

_____
_____

DAILY INTENTION

_____
_____

mindful morning

date:

TODAY I'M FEELING

_____

_____

_____

5 THINGS I'M GRATEFUL FOR

_____

_____

_____

_____

_____

DAILY AFFIRMATION

_____

_____

DAILY INTENTION

_____

_____

mindful morning

date:

TODAY I'M FEELING

_____
_____
_____

5 THINGS I'M GRATEFUL FOR

_____
_____
_____
_____
_____

DAILY AFFIRMATION

_____
_____

DAILY INTENTION

_____
_____

mindful morning

date:

TODAY I'M FEELING

_____
_____
_____

5 THINGS I'M GRATEFUL FOR

_____
_____
_____
_____
_____

DAILY AFFIRMATION

_____
_____

DAILY INTENTION

_____
_____

mindful morning

date:

TODAY I'M FEELING

_____
_____
_____

5 THINGS I'M GRATEFUL FOR

_____
_____
_____
_____
_____

DAILY AFFIRMATION

_____
_____

DAILY INTENTION

_____
_____

mindful morning

date:

TODAY I'M FEELING

_____
_____
_____

5 THINGS I'M GRATEFUL FOR

_____
_____
_____
_____
_____

DAILY AFFIRMATION

_____
_____

DAILY INTENTION

_____
_____

mindful morning

date:

TODAY I'M FEELING

_____
_____
_____

5 THINGS I'M GRATEFUL FOR

_____
_____
_____
_____
_____

DAILY AFFIRMATION

_____
_____

DAILY INTENTION

_____
_____

mindful morning

date:

TODAY I'M FEELING

_____
_____
_____

5 THINGS I'M GRATEFUL FOR

_____
_____
_____
_____
_____

DAILY AFFIRMATION

_____
_____

DAILY INTENTION

_____
_____

mindful morning

date:

TODAY I'M FEELING

_____
_____
_____

5 THINGS I'M GRATEFUL FOR

_____
_____
_____
_____
_____

DAILY AFFIRMATION

_____
_____

DAILY INTENTION

_____
_____

mindful morning

date:

TODAY I'M FEELING

_____
_____
_____

5 THINGS I'M GRATEFUL FOR

_____
_____
_____
_____
_____

DAILY AFFIRMATION

_____
_____

DAILY INTENTION

_____
_____

mindful morning

date:

TODAY I'M FEELING

_____
_____
_____

5 THINGS I'M GRATEFUL FOR

_____
_____
_____
_____
_____

DAILY AFFIRMATION

_____
_____

DAILY INTENTION

_____
_____

mindful morning

date:

TODAY I'M FEELING

_____
_____
_____

5 THINGS I'M GRATEFUL FOR

_____
_____
_____
_____
_____

DAILY AFFIRMATION

_____
_____

DAILY INTENTION

_____
_____

mindful morning

date:

TODAY I'M FEELING

_____
_____
_____

5 THINGS I'M GRATEFUL FOR

_____
_____
_____
_____
_____

DAILY AFFIRMATION

_____
_____

DAILY INTENTION

_____
_____

mindful morning

date:

TODAY I'M FEELING

_____

_____

_____

5 THINGS I'M GRATEFUL FOR

_____

_____

_____

_____

_____

DAILY AFFIRMATION

_____

_____

DAILY INTENTION

_____

_____

mindful morning

date:

TODAY I'M FEELING

_____
_____
_____

5 THINGS I'M GRATEFUL FOR

_____
_____
_____
_____
_____

DAILY AFFIRMATION

_____
_____

DAILY INTENTION

_____
_____

mindful morning

date:

TODAY I'M FEELING

_____
_____
_____

5 THINGS I'M GRATEFUL FOR

_____
_____
_____
_____
_____

DAILY AFFIRMATION

_____
_____

DAILY INTENTION

_____
_____

mindful morning

date:

TODAY I'M FEELING

_____
_____
_____

5 THINGS I'M GRATEFUL FOR

_____
_____
_____
_____
_____

DAILY AFFIRMATION

_____
_____

DAILY INTENTION

_____
_____

mindful morning

date:

TODAY I'M FEELING

_____
_____
_____

5 THINGS I'M GRATEFUL FOR

_____
_____
_____
_____
_____

DAILY AFFIRMATION

_____
_____

DAILY INTENTION

_____
_____

mindful morning

date:

TODAY I'M FEELING

_____
_____
_____

5 THINGS I'M GRATEFUL FOR

_____
_____
_____
_____
_____

DAILY AFFIRMATION

_____
_____

DAILY INTENTION

_____
_____

mindful morning

date:

TODAY I'M FEELING

_____

_____

_____

5 THINGS I'M GRATEFUL FOR

_____

_____

_____

_____

_____

DAILY AFFIRMATION

_____

_____

DAILY INTENTION

_____

_____

mindful morning

date:

TODAY I'M FEELING

_____
_____
_____

5 THINGS I'M GRATEFUL FOR

_____
_____
_____
_____
_____

DAILY AFFIRMATION

_____
_____

DAILY INTENTION

_____
_____

mindful morning

date:

TODAY I'M FEELING

_____
_____
_____

5 THINGS I'M GRATEFUL FOR

_____
_____
_____
_____
_____

DAILY AFFIRMATION

_____
_____

DAILY INTENTION

_____
_____

mindful morning

date:

TODAY I'M FEELING

_____
_____
_____

5 THINGS I'M GRATEFUL FOR

_____
_____
_____
_____
_____

DAILY AFFIRMATION

_____
_____

DAILY INTENTION

_____
_____

mindful morning

date:

TODAY I'M FEELING

_____
_____
_____

5 THINGS I'M GRATEFUL FOR

_____
_____
_____
_____
_____

DAILY AFFIRMATION

_____
_____

DAILY INTENTION

_____
_____

mindful morning

date:

TODAY I'M FEELING

_____
_____
_____

5 THINGS I'M GRATEFUL FOR

_____
_____
_____
_____
_____

DAILY AFFIRMATION

_____
_____

DAILY INTENTION

_____
_____

mindful morning

date:

TODAY I'M FEELING

_____
_____
_____

5 THINGS I'M GRATEFUL FOR

_____
_____
_____
_____
_____

DAILY AFFIRMATION

_____
_____

DAILY INTENTION

_____
_____

mindful morning

date:

TODAY I'M FEELING

_____
_____
_____

5 THINGS I'M GRATEFUL FOR

_____
_____
_____
_____
_____

DAILY AFFIRMATION

_____
_____

DAILY INTENTION

_____
_____

mindful morning

date:

TODAY I'M FEELING

_____

_____

_____

5 THINGS I'M GRATEFUL FOR

_____

_____

_____

_____

_____

DAILY AFFIRMATION

_____

_____

DAILY INTENTION

_____

_____

mindful morning

date:

TODAY I'M FEELING

_____
_____
_____

5 THINGS I'M GRATEFUL FOR

_____
_____
_____
_____
_____

DAILY AFFIRMATION

_____
_____

DAILY INTENTION

_____
_____

mindful morning

date:

TODAY I'M FEELING

_____
_____
_____

5 THINGS I'M GRATEFUL FOR

_____
_____
_____
_____
_____

DAILY AFFIRMATION

_____
_____

DAILY INTENTION

_____
_____

mindful morning

date:

TODAY I'M FEELING

_____
_____
_____

5 THINGS I'M GRATEFUL FOR

_____
_____
_____
_____
_____

DAILY AFFIRMATION

_____
_____

DAILY INTENTION

_____
_____

mindful morning

date:

TODAY I'M FEELING

_____
_____
_____

5 THINGS I'M GRATEFUL FOR

_____
_____
_____
_____
_____

DAILY AFFIRMATION

_____
_____

DAILY INTENTION

_____
_____

mindful morning

date:

TODAY I'M FEELING

_____

_____

_____

5 THINGS I'M GRATEFUL FOR

_____

_____

_____

_____

_____

DAILY AFFIRMATION

_____

_____

DAILY INTENTION

_____

_____

mindful morning

date:

TODAY I'M FEELING

_____
_____
_____

5 THINGS I'M GRATEFUL FOR

_____
_____
_____
_____
_____

DAILY AFFIRMATION

_____

DAILY INTENTION

_____
_____

mindful morning

date:

TODAY I'M FEELING

_____
_____
_____

5 THINGS I'M GRATEFUL FOR

_____
_____
_____
_____
_____

DAILY AFFIRMATION

_____
_____

DAILY INTENTION

_____
_____

mindful morning

date:

TODAY I'M FEELING

_____
_____
_____

5 THINGS I'M GRATEFUL FOR

_____
_____
_____
_____
_____

DAILY AFFIRMATION

_____
_____

DAILY INTENTION

_____
_____

mindful morning

date:

TODAY I'M FEELING

_____
_____
_____

5 THINGS I'M GRATEFUL FOR

_____
_____
_____
_____
_____

DAILY AFFIRMATION

_____
_____

DAILY INTENTION

_____
_____

mindful morning

date:

TODAY I'M FEELING

_____
_____
_____

5 THINGS I'M GRATEFUL FOR

_____
_____
_____
_____
_____

DAILY AFFIRMATION

_____
_____

DAILY INTENTION

_____
_____

mindful morning

date:

TODAY I'M FEELING

_____
_____
_____

5 THINGS I'M GRATEFUL FOR

_____
_____
_____
_____
_____

DAILY AFFIRMATION

_____
_____

DAILY INTENTION

_____
_____

mindful morning

date:

TODAY I'M FEELING

_____
_____
_____

5 THINGS I'M GRATEFUL FOR

_____
_____
_____
_____
_____

DAILY AFFIRMATION

_____
_____

DAILY INTENTION

_____
_____

mindful morning

date:

TODAY I'M FEELING

_____
_____
_____

5 THINGS I'M GRATEFUL FOR

_____
_____
_____
_____
_____

DAILY AFFIRMATION

_____
_____

DAILY INTENTION

_____
_____

mindful morning

date:

TODAY I'M FEELING

_____
_____
_____

5 THINGS I'M GRATEFUL FOR

_____
_____
_____
_____
_____

DAILY AFFIRMATION

_____
_____

DAILY INTENTION

_____
_____

mindful morning

date:

TODAY I'M FEELING

_____
_____
_____

5 THINGS I'M GRATEFUL FOR

_____
_____
_____
_____
_____

DAILY AFFIRMATION

_____
_____

DAILY INTENTION

_____
_____

mindful morning

date:

TODAY I'M FEELING

_____
_____
_____

5 THINGS I'M GRATEFUL FOR

_____
_____
_____
_____
_____

DAILY AFFIRMATION

_____
_____

DAILY INTENTION

_____
_____

Made in the USA
Columbia, SC
15 June 2021

40261339R00111